FOR
PARTLY PROUD
PARENTS

FOR PARTLY PROUD PARENTS

Light Verse about Children
by

RICHARD ARMOUR

With an Introduction by
PHYLLIS McGINLEY

Drawings by
LEO HERSHFIELD

HARPER & BROTHERS
Publishers / NEW YORK

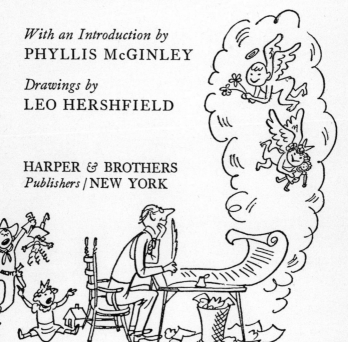

FOR PARTLY PROUD PARENTS

FIRST EDITION

TO
JEFF AND KARIN

ACKNOWLEDGMENTS

For permission to reprint certain of these poems which originally appeared in their pages, acknowledgment is gratefully made to the editors and publishers of *Better Homes and Gardens, Collier's, Good Housekeeping, The Saturday Evening Post, Today's Woman* and *Woman's Home Companion*.

INTRODUCTION
by
PHYLLIS McGINLEY

DURING the past fifteen years a good many eloquent people have talked a good deal of elegant nonsense about the Little People of the world. The Little People were forever in the headlines, stoically enduring, heroically resisting, or blandly upsetting elections.

I, for one, was never able really to envision a Little Person. He might be a midget, he might be a leprechaun; he certainly wasn't anybody I encountered on the subway or standing behind a counter.

Then enlightenment dawned. It dawned one rainy day when my house was particularly hideous with the patter of childish feet and the lilt of childish tantrums. I knew. The Little People, the submerged and driven and harried and voiceless inheritors of this earth, were Parents.

Everything was O.K. for children. Children were doing fine, riding high. They got bands on their teeth and vitamins in their lunch baskets and ten or eleven hours sleep a night. They got bicycles when the house needed new slip covers; and father and mother stayed home during vacation so that Junior could disport himself at summer camp. Children constituted the chief concern of nurses and educators and psychiatrists and comic-book publishers; and the moment they complained of headaches or homework, some champion came charging furiously to the rescue.

It was Parents who were the minority group. Who cared about them? Who was their spokesman? Was there a Society for the Prevention of Cruelty to Ancestors? Children and animals got protection, but not fathers and mothers. Did professors write books about how to overcome the frustration in forebears? Did the government pass laws regulating their hours of service? Was the nation deafened, blinded, drowned by advice (radio advice, magazine advice, the advice of educators and doctors and teachers and ordinary busybodies) on how to make parents happier and better integrated with their environment?

Not at all. Nobody, it seemed, dared to speak up for parents. They were forced to stumble along as best they could, cowed and humble, stifling their complaints. They got plenty of ordering about on how to do their jobs, but even that was an intolerable thing, for the orders kept changing monthly. One day parents would be told to feed Junior nothing but spinach—the next morning they'd find that spinach was considered completely unnecessary and should be abolished. As soon as they had digested the dictum from on high that babies should be picked up only at stated hours (on pain of ostracism from good society) another order would insist that babies be dandled only on demand from baby. Parents mustn't be severe.

They must be more severe. They should tell their charges the facts of life early. They mustn't speak of sex until they were spoken to. It is small wonder parents burnt out early, ending up as neurotics or in-laws or both, despised even by their progeny.

It was high time, I thought, that parents rose up in rebellion. Already they had lost their youth, their sleep, and their authority. What had they left to lose save their chains? They needed a Voice, and it had not spoken.

I was too pessimistic. Unknown to me, at that very moment, on a California campus, a voice was being lifted.

It was not the voice of an agitator—of a Robespierre or a Trotsky. It was a mild and patient and reasonable voice. It did not advocate abolishing children. It did not recommend overthrowing (bloodily) the Progressive School. Rather, it sought to explain the case of Parents. It asserted that they, too, had beating hearts and palpitating nerves and Rights.

The voice belonged to one Richard Armour, doubly one of the Little People, because in addition to being a Parent he was also a Poet. And this book is his manifesto.

How he managed to smuggle the subversive document out of the state, notorious as the blackest example of Parent-subservience, I do not know. (No doubt there is already a price on his head.) But perhaps there exists a better organized Underground than we realize. At any rate the verses did get into the hands of a sympathetic and freedom-loving publisher, and this volume is the result.

Parents who read (and they say there are many such, although they do it by night and stealthily) can now see themselves presented in a properly sympathetic light. What deflated father, what exhausted mother, but must applaud the poignant lines:

> But nevertheless, when the day is done
> And at last in bed is my little son,
> It isn't the twig that is bent, I sigh,
> It is I.

Or the moving words of "On the Phase of It."

> My child is "going through a phase."
> I should rejoice, but curse.
> In many ways
> I like this phase—
> The next one *may* be worse!

Even the younger generation must recognize themselves here, and if they don't burn the book in the streets (or, more likely, use it to crack nuts on the parquet floor) may give thought to what lies ahead. For Armour is Telling All, he is Striking a Blow, but he is also a merciful man. Even at his most cutting, he has the welfare of the race at heart. Adults must rise up all right, he warns. But this book contains another sort of warning, an implicit one, and it is this: Let every child remember that he too may some day join the ranks of the underprivileged. Some day he, too, may be a Parent.

FOR
PARTLY PROUD
PARENTS

MINIATURE

My DAY-OLD son is plenty scrawny,
His mouth is wide with screams, or yawny,
His ears seem larger than he's needing,
His nose is flat, his chin's receding,
His skin is very very red,
He has no hair upon his head,
And yet I'm proud as proud can be
To hear you say he looks like me.

HOW MUCH DID BABY EAT?

Subtract, as well as you are able,
The dabs and dribs upon the table;
Deduct the morsels on the floor
And in the chair, and what is more—
Although of this we hate to speak—
Allow for food on chin and cheek.
Then what's not on the outside maybe
Has somehow got inside of Baby.

NOCTURNE

WHEN the baby cries at night,
It is I who lights the light.
It is I who notes the hour
Baby stirs within his bower.

It is I who wonders if
What we heard was cough or sniff,
Possibly, if it were cough,
Meaning bedclothes might be off.

It is I who calls to mind
Tales of most depressing kind:
Smotherings and such as that,
Breath sucked out by alley cat,

Kidnapings and kindred harm.
It is I who sounds alarm.
It is I who well advises
My dear wife, who then arises!

TO A BAWLING BABE

STOP that yelling, screaming, yowling.
Cease that heart-is-breaking howling.
What's a pinprick? What's some damp?
Dry your eyes, you little scamp.

Wait till you've had more of life,
Got a job, some debts, a wife,
Then, I haven't any doubt,
You'll have things to cry about!

'TWAS THE NIGHT (LATE)
BEFORE CHRISTMAS

'Twas the night before Christmas, and all through
the house
Two creatures were stirring—just me and my
spouse.
To attic and cellar we secretly sped
As soon as the children lay safely in bed,
And in many a closet, as busy as elves,
Pulled down all the parcels stacked high on the
shelves.

We brought in the tree, which we found much too
tall,
And we topped it and lopped it and stopped it from
fall;
We tore up some boxes and badly behaved
While seeking the tinsel we *thought* we had saved.
And then, upon chairs and with foothold pre-
carious,
We hung up our ornaments many and various.

The tree now resplendent, except for the fact
That the lights wouldn't light (a connection we
lacked),
We filled up the stockings—a job not done quickly—

And vacuumed the rugs, which were tinseled so
    thickly,
And then, when we'd read and reread the direc-
    tions,
Assembled the toys that had come all in sections.

The hour was now midnight and quite a bit past,
But our labors, thank Heaven, were finished at
    last. . . .
As we gazed at our efforts through lead-lidded
    eyes
And thought of the morrow and shouts of surprise,
We prayed that the children, on the morn of St.
    Nick's,
Would please not awaken at least until six!

NO SOONER SAID

WANT to know how we get our recalcitrant son
To do what he balks at, but ought to be done?
How we make him plunge into the task full of zest
And not only do it, but do it his best,
And even feel gloatingly glad that he did it?
We forbid it!

SOMETHING TO COUNT ON

I TELL my son that he must do
The thing he balks at, and be through—
Wash hands and face, or eat his food,
Or say he's sorry he was rude,
Or put his coat on when it's cold,
Or do whatever he's been told,
And do it there and do it then—
Before I count from one to ten.

But I know well that I'll go slow
When I have got to six or so,
That I'll expectantly await
A change of heart—good boy!—by eight,
And that I'll patiently resign
Myself to other means at nine.

I know, alas, what I shall do,
And what is more, he knows it, too!

HOUSE A-BUILDING

JUNGLES have pythons
  And swamps have adders,
But the house a-building
  Has shaky ladders.

In the ocean the shark
  With the sting-ray mingles,
But the house a-building
  Has falling shingles.

Golf balls carom
  On golf course fairways,
But the house a-building
  Has open stairways.

The house a-building
  Has oil for oiling
And glass that's brittle
  And tar that's boiling;

It's full of perils
  And means of slaughter—
And you'll find there daily
  My son and daughter!

DIVIDED WE FALTER

Should our offspring get a whaling
    Or a kiss upon the cheek?
Is our resolution failing,
    Are we stern or are we weak?

Should we use soft soap or switch, dear,
    To achieve our hoped-for aim?
It's of little moment which, dear,
    If we both just do the same!

COMMON CARRIER

A BOY can bring so much outdoors
    Indoors, on clothes and hide,
It really is a wonder that
    There's any left outside.

DEFORMATIVE YEARS

As THE twig is bent—so the saying goes,
And I do my darnedest, goodness knows.
But nevertheless, when the day is done
And at last in bed is my little son,
It isn't the twig that is bent, I sigh,
It is I.

BAD ACTORS

Is YOUR young hopeful shy and dumb
   When company is present?
And does he sit and suck his thumb
   In manner most unpleasant?

Well, I've a child who'll romp and rant,
   Who dotes on entertaining,
And for the life of me I can't
   See why *you* are complaining!

TO A YOUNG LADY AGED SIX

I THOUGHT I could not love you more
When you were three, when you were four.

It seemed that one could not contrive
More loveliness than you at five.

But now, a thing of slender grace,
With eager freshness in your face,

There is no doubt that you reveal
A devastating six appeal.

ON THE PHASE OF IT

My CHILD is "going through a phase."
  I should rejoice, but curse.
In many ways
I like this phase—
  The next one *may* be worse!

REPORT CARD RECEIVED

My BOY is doing well in school:
He minds, he never breaks a rule;
He loves his work so much, he stays
An extra hour or two, some days;
He's quick to learn, nor soon forgets,
In fact, he's one of teacher's pets.

Or so I thought, from what he told me,
But what a bill of goods he sold me!

UNREQUIRED READING

Junior is learning to read, these days,
    He's plowing his way through a primer,
And though his performance is nothing to praise,
    He's showing an average glimmer.

Yes, Junior is learning to read for himself,
    But I almost wish that he wouldn't,
For all too soon he'll be at my shelf,
    Reading the things he shouldn't.

HOME GUARD

Against my will I was dragged out
   And at a party find me,
Where ruefully I muse about
   The girl I left behind me.

And as the evening wears (and wears),
   I hourly grow more bitter
To think of how my lot compares
   With hers—the baby sitter.

She is the mistress of my home
   As soon as I've departed.
Not made, like me, perforce to roam,
   She reads the book I'd started.

Upon the radio she hears
   The programs I am missing.
My records, gathered through the years,
   She plays, while reminiscing.

While I hide yawns as best I can
   At talk not of my choosing,
She stretches out on my divan
   And does a little snoozing.

But what is just too much for me
    And turns me really sour
Is that it isn't I, but she,
    Who gets paid by the hour!

IS THERE A BABY IN THE HOUSE?

A HOME without a baby
Is a hive without a bee,
A nest without a robin,
A pod without a pea,
A rainbow lacking color,
A summer with no heat,
An ocean still and saltless,
A heart that doesn't beat.

A home that has a baby
Is a busy, buzzing hive,
A pod that's full to bursting,
A nest that is alive,
A many-colored rainbow,
A summer's warmest part,
A wavy, salty ocean,
A steady beating heart.

CYCLE

JUNIOR gets a cold somewhere,
His sister gets it next;
The end, however, isn't there,
And that's what makes us vexed.

For Sister's cold is passed on then
To Father and to Mother,
Who barely have recovered when—
Yes, Junior gets another!

INNOCENCE ABROAD

My boy was innocent and pure,
   Knew nothing really bad,
Until—of this I'm very sure—
   He met the neighbor lad.

The neighbor lad's the wicked one,
   The thorn upon the vine.
How strange, my neighbors think their son
   Learned what he knows from mine!

THE PARENTS' HOUR

I LOVE to dress my little boy
　　And help him with his meals,
I love to fix his broken toy
　　And have him at my heels.

I love to romp upon the floor
　　And read his story book,
And imitate the lion's roar
　　And watch his raptured look.

I love to answer, as he asks,
　　His thousand daily questions,
And guide him in his little tasks
　　With actions and suggestions.

I love to bathe him, feet to head,
　　But what I love the best,
Is tucking him, at last, in bed,
　　So I can get some rest!

SUCCESS!

AT LAST my child says "please" and "thank you"
    Without his being told to.
Of course the lad is grown and married,
    And I am pretty old too.

PRETTY AS WHAT PICTURE?

One's an angel, one's a minx,
One child beams, the other blinks,
One's all set, but one's not ready,
One is wiggling, one is steady,
One exhibits all the graces,
The other's busy making faces....

Might as well reach down a star,
Walk on water, stop a war,
Order rain or sunny weather,
As photograph two kids together.

RAISING THE QUESTION

When I grow vexed and weary
  From Junior's ceaseless "Why?"
His morn-to-evening query
  About the earth and sky,

My nerves are nearly shattered,
  My patience flickers low,
But how my ego's flattered
  To think he'd think I know!

DEFLATION

Sons and daughters
In their teens
Think their parents
Don't know beans.

Which would not be
Hard to face
Were it not so
Oft the case.

HELP!

Our child, when small, would beg and beg
    To dust or set the table
Or bake a pie. Unhappily,
    She wasn't able.

At last our child is big enough
    To be a table setter
Or do a dozen helpful things—
    But try and get her!

GOINGS ON

Not "five," says the parent, but "going on six,"
    Not "six," but "going on seven."
A child is ten for a day, and then—
    That's right, "going on eleven."

But find me the parent of thirty-nine
    Sufficiently candid and sporty
To come right out with a good clear shout—
    "Me? I'm going on forty!"

MIND OVER MANNERS

A PORTION of a woman's days
    Most pleasantly is whiled
By thinking of the *other* ways
    She'd raise her neighbor's child.

RECOGNITION

IF YOU'RE thinking of fame
And a recognized name,
   I warn you right now not to bother.
Till your life is half done
You're your father's son,
   And then you become your son's father.

NUMBERS GAME

Here is a problem
I never enjoy—
Given: two children,
Given: one toy.

CANCELED OUT

I STUDIED a volume on bringing up children
And got all the answers to questions bewild'rin'.

I underlined passages, jotted down notes,
And memorized specially meaningful quotes.

I gleaned many pointers indeed, and the fact is,
Was just about ready to put them in practice

When, reading a volume more recent and long,
I found that the first one was utterly wrong.

PULLING NO PUNCHES

WHAT an awful beating kids
  Would get (the thought allures),
If you could whale the neighbors' brats
  And they could punish yours!

DOING ALL RIGHT

THE child today lags far behind,
   He's lazy and he's dumb,
     You rant;
But can you make a yo-yo wind,
   Can *you* blow bubble gum?
     I can't!

EAR MARKS OF A BOY

At times my son has got me fearing
He might, perhaps, be hard of hearing.
When out at play, although I call
He doesn't seem to hear at all,
And when I say, "Go wash your hands,"
Or "Put your toys away," he stands
Around as if he hadn't heard
A single solitary word.

It's only when I tell his mother
Some whispered little thing or other
I'd just as soon he wouldn't learn,
I find his hearing's no concern.

THE WAY IT WORKS OUT

THE parents who do not believe in spanking
   These days are a numerous host,
And the worst of it is, they're the parents of kids
   Who, the rest of us think, need it most!

DISTANCE LENDS ENCHANTMENT

Do THE children upset you?
    Are they turning you gray?
The solution's quite simple:
    Just up and away.

Then, once you are distant,
    Well out of their range,
Observe the remarkable,
    Wonderful change.

Forgetting their badness,
    The difficult days,
You're showing their photos
    To all who will gaze.

Horns become halos,
    The noise is a tune,
And you can't hie you homeward
    A minute too soon!

TWICE ME

My son is such a little me—
I wonder, sometimes, if it's he
Or one like him I used to know
And be, in fact, some years ago.

Sometimes it is not father, son.
Sometimes I feel like two, not one.
The self of now, the self of then. . . .
Time, overlapping, doubles men.

ONE MORE

ONE more story,
One more game,
Then we'll scamper—
So they claim.

One more giant,
One more jump,
Off to bed
They say they'll hump....

One's so few
It's hardly any—
Strange one more
Can be so many!

WONDERLAND

Today a jungle, dark and deep,
Through which intrepid hunters creep
And, rifles poised, undaunted dare
The lion lurking in his lair;
Tomorrow, strangely gone all trace
Of jungle, this once teeming place
Becomes a plain where last-ditch stand
Is made against the redskin band;
Or yet again, a battlefield
Where cannons roar and tanks are wheeled
Until at last the riddled foe
Retreats, with tattered ensigns low;
Or, neither jungle, field, nor plain,
An island in the Spanish Main,
Where earringed pirates, rough and bold,
Exhume the long-hid chest of gold. . . .

Yet grownups, in their purblind way,
Can look, unseeing, day by day,
And still insist this magic spot
Is nothing but a vacant lot.

CHILDREN

One day they're angels, lacking only wings,
The next, they're puppets to the Devil's strings.

One day they do precisely as they're told,
Nor need be threatened, beaten, or cajoled;
The next, despite all switchings, bribes, and talk,
Like little mules they obstinately balk.
One day they're unobtrusive, out of sight,
No slightest trouble from the morn till night;
The next, in their inimitable way,
They're underfoot, and screaming, all the day.
One day they keep their face and clothing clean,
For hours and hours preserve that washtub sheen;
The next, as straight as arrows shot from bow,
To mud or grease or jam or paint they go.
One day, in other words, you love and praise them,
The next, you wonder how you'll ever raise them.

One day they're angels, sent to you from heaven.
But what's one day, I ask you, out of seven?

Set in Linotype Caslon Old Face
Format by A. W. Rushmore
Manufactured by The Haddon Craftsmen
Published by HARPER & BROTHERS
New York